Presented to

_____

_____

by

_____

_____

To Love and to Cherish

Roy G. Gesch

CONCORDIA

Publishing House
St. Louis

Other Books by Roy G. Gesch:

CONFIRMED IN CHRIST

GOD'S WORLD THROUGH YOUNG EYES

HELP! I'M IN COLLEGE

A HUSBAND PRAYS/A WIFE PRAYS

Scripture quotations are from The Holy Bible: NEW INTER-NATIONAL VERSION, Copyright © 1978 by the New York International Bible Society. Used by permission of Zondervan Bible Publishers.

Copyright © 1985 by Concordia Publishing House,
3558 South Jefferson Avenue, St. Louis, MO 63118-3968.
Manufactured in the United States of America.

Library of Congress Cataloging in Publication Data

Gesch, Roy G.
        To love and to cherish.

        1. Marriage—Religious aspects—Christianity.
I. Title.
BV835.G47   1985   248.8'4   84-15634
ISBN 0-570-04214-3 (pbk.)

1 2 3 4 5 6 7 8 9 10   DB   94 93 92 91 90 89 88 87 86 85

To my beloved Dorothy,
with whom I have found the joy
of quality in marriage.

CONTENTS

FOREWORD

There is no lack of advice or advisers when two people get married. And seldom are two people more interested in good advice than when they are about to enter a relationship as unique and promising as marriage. Most couples standing at the altar and vowing enduring devotion to each other can use all the help they can get.

Christian men and women are fortunate to be able to turn to the most reliable source for marital counseling: to the Designer and Creator of marriage—to God Himself in His Word. There the Originator of love reveals how His human creatures can capture and enjoy a loving relationship as long as they live.

To Love and to Cherish shows the Christian bride and groom how to build a lasting relationship according to God's blueprint in the Scriptures. Following those directions will all but guarantee a blessed union—which is another name for a truly happy marriage.

This book is meant to make that wish come true for you.

—THE PUBLISHER

"I DO!"

I do!" That's an interesting phrase, is it not?

You use that phrase in so many ways every day because you do so many different things each day.

Yet when you hear that phrase all by itself, it conjures up the picture of two people very much in love with each other, standing hand in hand, looking into each other's eyes warmly and tenderly, pledging undying companionship and faithfulness to each other.

"I do!" conveys an air of excitement. Much joyous anticipation and much careful preparation precede that precious moment when those simple words of commitment are spoken. It is a type of anticipation and preparation that is unlike any other. For there is no other statement or commitment that so fully involves the entire person for so long a time in so meaningful a way.

*Y*ou also have spoken those words. You have experienced that choice moment in your life.

When you said "I do!", you were not just mouthing words to comply with legal marriage requirements. Those two little words were intended and spoken as a promise. You entered willingly and joyously into a mutual agreement with the one you loved above all others. You chose from that day forward to invest your life—your time, your love, your energies—in your togetherness. You set a course to face life side by side.

What brought you to the point that you were ready to make such a momentous and significant commitment?

To say you fell in love is certainly an understatement. It is true, of course! But when you stop to think about it, there's something strangely, almost mysteriously wonderful about what we call love.

Why do you have those special feelings for that one person? You've been rubbing elbows and sharing delightful experiences with dozens of people all your life. You've built up a little group of special friends. There are many who have something special, and you admire them for their outstanding traits and abilities.

Yet you settled in on one. And simultaneously—and that is also part of the wonder of it all—that person zeroed in on you. Then after months, perhaps even years—hopefully more than weeks—of careful deliberation and discussion, you made the decision. And the day finally came when you promised lifelong love and fidelity to each other in the presence of family and friends.

Was it body chemistry? just an accident?

It makes far more sense to recognize that God, in His love for us, has a wonderful plan for each of our lives. Marriage and family are part of a personal enrichment program designed by God.

The same God who drafted the blueprint for marriage is the God who designed humans in the first place. He made us as we are—complete!

—physical beings with strength and beauty and with the ability to procreate and recreate;

—emotional beings with the capacity to feel and love, to attract and be attracted;

—rational beings able to think and discern, to dream and plan;

—beings with a spiritual dimension, who can sense the Creator's presence in their daily lives, gain understanding through His revelation in His Word, and draw on His guidance and power.

It's no accident that you found each other—or that you found in each other what you were looking for in a life companion.

If you know God at all, you can recognize His love and direction in bringing you together. But God is more than a divine Matchmaker. He is rather the One who made you for each other.

That's doubly significant in view of the times in which we live.

It used to be that people took marriage for granted. If two people loved each other, they got married. That was the normal course. Marriage seemed the ideal answer to personal needs and problems.

More recently marriage has been challenged. Undiscerning folk lumped marriage together with a host of so-called outmoded traditions. The alarming divorce rate—almost half the number of marriages performed each year—caused some to suggest naively that marriage was the cause of divorce, that all the unhappiness experienced in severed unions could be avoided by not creating those unions in the first place.

That of course immediately became the platform for the ever-present irresponsible playboy and playgirl who wanted sex without commitment, sex without love, sex without marriage. "Living together" was the substitute proposal. In that way "I'm free to be me!" with no shackles on personal freedom. If things didn't work out, or if you became disillusioned, you could just walk out. There were no strings attached, no legal paper contract and all the hassle involved in changing status afterwards, no potential haggling over the division of property. You could find out if you really did love each other. If it worked, you could still get married afterwards. If not, nothing was lost.

But that was yesterday too. People who opted to live together soon discovered that their stresses were no different from those of married couples.

They hurt just as much and had just as many problems and ill feelings when they separated. "Palimony" was devised to replace the averted alimony. People learned that marriage was not the culprit. *They* were the problem. It was still all a matter of human relationships.

Most recent public opinion surveys show that the pendulum has swung in the other direction again. The trend is back to more traditional values. People need a sense of commitment, the ability to trust and rely on one another.

The numbers may differ from poll to poll. They depend on the audience being tested, who does the testing, when it takes place, and the latitude of the questions. But the results are basically the same.

One survey conducted by a family magazine revealed that 88 percent of those responding were satisfied with their marriages. Eighty percent said that nothing in their lives was as important as their family. That is truly significant when you consider the importance most people place on career, social position, standard of living, and material possessions.

While those figures may be viewed as high because of the nature of the publication conducting the survey, they correspond with the results of other polls. A broader survey revealed that 96 percent of those questioned were making New Year resolutions to improve their family life. Why were they so concerned about family? Why were others so satisfied with their marriages? What elements contributed most to their happiness?

While "children" topped the list, most of the varying answers focused on "closeness" and "loving companionship." Togetherness in religion and in helping one another, doing things with and for each other, and the ability to communicate and understand, appreciate and respect each other were also cited as truly important.

Of course, that's not the impression you get from the media. Many television situation comedies and dramas and many sensationalized magazine articles still play around the edges. They are convinced that sex sells. And so their story lines still suggest that morality is changing, and that marriage is passé and in deep trouble.

But feel good about this—your simple love and wholehearted commitment are not really going against the grain of contemporary society. And anyway, what if you are out of step? Real treasures are not mass-produced. They are a cut above the ordinary. They take on tremendous value just because they are special, perhaps even to the point of being a rarity.

That's the kind of marriage you want!

And that's the kind of marriage you can have and will have if you go at your marriage God's way—and stick with it His way.

In spite of how the winds of change may blow, in spite of the conditioning pressures of society and friends around you, you can have a truly good marriage. And you can anticipate full joy and blessing together through all the years ahead.

That's the way God designed it—also for you!

I do!" Do you remember when you spoke those words to each other?

There was a strange mixture of feelings at that moment.

On the one hand, there was that genuine feeling of love. You really wanted to make the promise, and you really wanted to keep that promise. And you were so happy to know that your chosen life partner felt the same way.

On the other hand, there were those little nagging doubts and concerns: Am I really ready for this? It's going to mean a total change in my life. Are we really right for each other?

You had been reasonably sure of yourselves, but those last-minute preparations for the wedding were a bit unsettling. Differences of opinion surfaced as never before when families and friends began to take over the wedding plans. What had seemed like such a simple, beautiful, and meaningful act suddenly got entangled with all the trappings of a ceremonial pageant—rituals and proprieties—the big event of the season.

As family differences and preferences became apparent, family loyalties were demonstrated by the bride and groom. The fun was going out of it. Was this a taste of the realities of the future?

But slipping away for a few private quiet times of talking and praying put everything back into perspective. Those nagging doubts were pretty much dissolved by the love you shared.

In those few moments before the altar, you suddenly realized again that this was it! "Can anyone here present show just cause why these two should not be united in holy wedlock?" Surely no one would—or even could! But could we? Were we really sure of ourselves? There was to be no turning back after this moment.

You didn't turn back. You did it! As you looked into each other's eyes and whispered "I do," all else faded into insignificant background. This was it—the moment you'd been waiting and planning for! The two of you made the commitment to go forward into the rest of life together.

You did it! And you were glad!

I do!" Do what?

"I take you to be my wedded spouse." A new relationship was established. A man and a woman became a husband and a wife. New roles were assumed. You were both committing yourselves to something neither of you was before.

But one does not truly become something merely by choosing a new title. The person who

says, "I want to be a doctor," does not thereby
become a doctor, nor does anyone in any profession
or role. There is a lot to learn first before one truly
qualifies.

Yet in marriage it was a little different. "On the
basis of your promises, sincerely and truly spoken,
I now pronounce you husband and wife." That's
what the preacher said. And from then on everyone
looked on you and treated you as husband and
wife—"Mr. and Mrs."

Husband and wife—on the basis of a promise,
not a diploma. The learning in marriage all lay
ahead. It was to be totally on-the-job training.

But it is not walking a blind path. You soon
discovered the way was filled with excellent ex-
amples of others who had made and were still making beautiful marriages. You knew you could
emulate them. If necessary, you could even go to
them for counsel and advice.

*M*oreover, you had perfect guidelines regard-
ing marriage and marriage roles laid out by
God for you in His Word. The Designer and Creator also spelled out all the standards. He provided
you with a user's manual that came with explicit
instructions and a lifetime warranty.

Like all user's manuals, it warns that unless
proper steps of maintenance are used and adjustments and repairs made when they are needed,
the warranty will not apply. Nor are there any as-

surances of customer satisfaction if the product—in this case marriage—is abused.

In His marriage manual, the Designer begins by saying that the original design—man—is good. He fits into the whole scheme of creation in a truly wonderful way. But the Designer saw fit to add an improvement to the picture through the addition of woman.

This provided a level of complete and fulfilling companionship that did not exist before. Best of all, God did not provide a companion who was an exact copy. Rather He provided a complementary companion.

The two were designed to be similar, yet different from each other—physically, emotionally, mentally, and even spiritually. It's not that either was, or was ever meant to be, superior to the other. They would complete each other. Woman was described as a "helper suitable" for man (Gen. 2:18). And very truly, in the same sense, man is found to be a "helper suitable" for her. They fulfill each other.

In the light of this background, the simple Scripture directives on marriage come through most logically and beautifully. The ultimate in complementing and completing each other comes about as the two become one.

Each leaves all others, including father and mother, to establish a singular relationship with that one other. As Jesus stated it, "The two will become one flesh. So they are no longer two, but one" (Matt. 19:5-6).

By design it is a complete oneness—one flesh, one heart, one mind. It is not two people in a lamination or two sharing the same household space. The two have merged their lives, invested them in each other. They have merged their futures, their goals, and their dreams and have chosen to share each other's burdens and cares.

When you stated publicly, "I take you," you were not conforming to tradition. Customs vary by place and culture. This had nothing to do with either custom or culture. Nor was it a formal step to gain the right to intimacies that had been previously restricted or forbidden.

You were entering the primal human relationship. You were doing it on the basis of God's guidelines. And you were doing it in joyous expectation of His blessings.

For what it is worth to you, let me assure you that you did a good thing. If you follow through in God's way on what you began His way, you have every reason to anticipate a blessed marriage and a happy home.

Chapter 2

"WE DO!"

I do!" That simple promissory statement was good as far as it went. But remember—the promise is only the beginning of the picture, the first stroke on the canvas.

One of the first adjustments in marriage—and incidentally, one of the hardest to make—is the change in thought pattern from "I" to "we."

That's understandable. Until now there has been a perfectly natural focus on "I." Even when there were siblings in the family, there was a certain amount of fending for oneself. At least to a degree, you had to look out for yourself. You learned how to become self-reliant and self-determining. You planned your future and selected the schools and courses that would best prepare you for a vocation. You wrote resumes and submitted job applications. You had to sell yourself, to convince others that you were the person they were looking for.

To do that, you had to be sold on yourself. You had to come to realize that God made you to be a somebody. You had worth. You were worth developing. You had a future with promise.

In a sense, this spilled over into courtship too. You found the person you deemed the best of them all—at least the best for you. Now you went to great lengths to convince that person that you were worth the risk of marriage.

All along there has been a tremendous emphasis on self. And that feeling of self-worth or self-respect must continue in marriage if marriage is to meet its full potential.

*B*ut an overemphasis on self can and will lead to the erosion and washout of marriage. We all have seen far too much of that, especially in recent years.

We are still emerging from what has been called the "Me Generation." Marriage was one of the major casualties of that philosophical struggle. "I need more space to find out who I really am" is the way some put it. "Marriage does not permit me to be free to be me." "I was so crowded in marriage that I never did get my head on straight."

It is sad that some potentially good marriages never materialized because they were never given a chance. Many were misled—and many still are—into believing that self-gratification is the key to happiness and fulfillment. What an irretrievable loss it is when a person discovers too late that true fulfillment is to be found in the unselfish sharing of love and self. It does not—and cannot—lie in putting self first.

*T*he key to a good marriage lies in balancing the "I" and the "we." The "I do!" in marriage is a good formula because one person is not saying it alone. The two are making identical commitments to each other. The "I do!" has become "We do!"

"We take each other." That's the start of true oneness. It is the beginning of living together, working together, praying together, playing together, planning together, setting goals and working towards those goals together, establishing priorities together.

The two have become one—a oneness that you both will nurture and protect over the years to come. A oneness that, by God's grace and your continued efforts, will continue to grow with the passing of time.

The "I's" have become the "we"—we together, each a whole person, each still free to be me, but not at the other's expense!

Chapter 3

"WE WILL!"

*I*t is pretty clear that the "We do!" is the easy part of marriage—perhaps too easy.

Attraction, infatuation, and love can be like a stream that moves you ever closer to the altar. At first the movement is almost imperceptible. When you do become aware of it, you are enjoying yourself so much, you do not want to change the course. So the days of dating drift into days of dreaming and planning.

The initial steps of planning deal more with fluff than anything substantial. It's a time of exploring each other's likes and dislikes, going places, having fun together, looking for any excuse to be together again.

But a lot more planning, and planning of a more substantial nature, is needed. Hopefully the fun and games give way to much more serious matters—to the realities that make up most of life.

When that does not happen, you end up with people of high potential in their twenties and thirties, disillusioned over marriage and family. Their familiar lament is heard across the land: "I was too young when I got married!" "We really were not ready for marriage!"

And they are right! They really were not ready! "Get ready" and "Get set" must precede "Go."

Marriage is not much different from any other major step in life. If you are going to tie yourself down to a long-term commitment, you had better be sure what you are doing.

A young man or woman enters medical school. TV has done a good job of glamorizing the medical profession, depicting the young medic as today's knight in shining armor. Night after night, in episode after episode, appealing interns and nurses charge out into exciting new adventures to snatch people from the jaws of death. They then go on to enjoy the adulation and undying gratitude of loyal patients and appreciative families. Sure they lose one occasionally. But in the final scene they can usually settle down comfortably together with a glass of wine and soft lights and music over a quiet dinner.

Now there's the good life! You can feel you are doing something worthwhile. You are fighting death and disease! You are helping people! And you are rewarded so handsomely for it! You have a good income—sufficient to enable an early and secure retirement!

So it's off to medical school. You discover it involves unbelievably hard work and long hours— years of demanding personal sacrifices. During internship you also discover that much of the future will be unbelievably monotonous and routine.

And people do not always respond to your care and treatment. Patients may be more complaining than appreciative. You find yourself getting more and more depressed, and you can't stand being around sick people all the time.

What a waste! When approaching a career, it is imperative to face up to realities and know what you are getting into before you get there.

That's true in approaching a marriage too!

The same basics apply when buying a house. You walk through a new development. A few model units are open for inspection. The developer has hired the best local interior decorator to furnish them beautifully.

The model is everything you dreamed of in your home. It's small, true! But look how much you can do with so little space.

Mirrored walls and mirrored closet doors give the feel of openness to even the smallest rooms. Converting a closet into a desk alcove, complete with cabinets and bookshelves, is an attractive space-saver. A variety of wood paneling and a limitless selection of wallpapers are available to give any room any look you want. You hardly even notice the decals that clearly state that these are all decorator items, not included in the price, or that the grade of carpeting in the models is not the standard grade the home buyer will receive. Nor do you envision the furniture you have in contrast to the elegant pieces on display.

What about the quality of the standard wall and roofing materials? or the workmanship in the bare units? or the plumbing and electrical systems? What about the drainage in the yard?

Can you meet the down payment? Can you afford the monthly payments, the taxes and insurance? Will you be so strapped you will never have the money to make all those nice little upgrades and improvements that sold you on the house in the first place?

Is it well located? Or will you need a second car immediately? Can you afford that? Once you sign the papers, you are really locked in.

It really is important that everyone assess the cost and examine the realities of married life before agreeing to make the promise. That's why most ministers and counselors offer and urge some type of "Getting Ready for Marriage" program.

Things will really change. As a single person you are free to do what you want any time. You can buy what you want and spend as much as you choose for it. You can indulge in your own type of entertainment, sports, and hobbies. You do not have to adjust for or account to anyone else. You set your own scale of priorities.

It's different in marriage. The same options are still open, but the new perspective is to determine what WE need and what WE want and what WE feel will be most beneficial to our home and family.

Before making the promise, it is necessary to face up to this. Do I know the personal cost? Am I willing to pay that price? Am I ready to assume that responsibility? Am I willing to put "us" above "me"? Am I mature enough to handle it?

The "We do!" is deceptively easy. The "We will!" is not.

The key to a good marriage lies in the "We will!" That's the real heart of the promise and of the marriage.

What are the elements of that promise? The wording or formulas may vary with the ceremony, but they are all essentially the same.

"We will" love each other, honor and respect each other, comfort and uphold each other. "We will" pledge our faithfulness to each other for as long as God gives us life. "We will" keep this sacred and close bond holy and unbroken. "We will" live together and work together in sickness and in health, in poverty and wealth, no matter how the times and tides of life may turn against us.

That's the promise you made to each other, the commitment you each took upon yourself. So help you God!

That's quite a promise! Let's look at it more carefully.

A man will leave his father and mother and be united to his wife" is the way Jesus put it when He was questioned about marriage (Matt. 19:5). But God's blueprints show that there is much more to marriage than breaking parental ties and launching out on one's own.

"Forsaking all others" is the way one wedding rite puts it. That special oneness you two have established is different from all other present and future relationships. You took a new responsibility on yourselves. You no longer have the same responsibility to anyone else. You owe it solely to each other.

It is simplistic and insufficient to say that this means it is wrong to sleep around, to have an affair, or to have a secret longing to share such intimacies with anyone else. The promise is positive. By God's grace you have found so much in each other that you cannot even conceive of the same happiness with anyone else. Nor do you even want to entertain the idea of seeking such happiness elsewhere.

Leaving all others means that you have committed yourselves to growing and maturing in your relationship to the point where you know you can depend on one another at all times and in all situations. You don't go running home to mother, because you don't feel the need. You've been growing together so well that you can stay and work things out together. You don't have to pour out your intimate heartaches to your neighbors or co-workers, because you have been learning how to talk things through with each other.

W e pledge our faithfulness in every duty" is another facet of the promise. And it brings up another key word—*duty*.

Commitment brings duty and responsibility.

Before marriage you may have been impressed, even overwhelmed, by the thoughtfulness, considerateness, and helpfulness you saw in the one you love. You appreciate these traits equally as much in marriage, and you intend never to take them for granted. But in marriage you need to be able to depend on those virtues. There would be a void if suddenly they were not there.

What may be options and niceties outside marriage become duties in marriage. You must know what foundations you are building on. And you must have confidence that they are dependable and strong enough so that together you can weather whatever storms may arise in years ahead.

T he "We will!" is a commitment to stay together—"not to part from you as long as God gives us life," "till death do us part."

That's a big order. What if . . .?

It's obvious that many people have considered it too big. Despite their best of intentions, they reached a breaking point. "I just couldn't take it anymore!" The soaring divorce rate and unregistered separations are public evidence that there are many all around us who felt they could take no more. Their life together just was not what they had expected it to be. "We were bad for each other. The longer we were together, the more miserable we were."

There's no denying that many are happier in separation than they were in marriage. And many second marriages are better than the first because they "are not making the same mistakes."

Is the lifelong commitment too demanding then? Is it unrealistic in terms of the pressures encountered in today's fast-paced world?

Some who have written their own ceremonies have deleted that phrase. They have expressed the feeling that lifelong fidelity is a beautiful ideal, and they sincerely hope that it will work out that way for them. But it is not a promise, not a binding commitment.

Yet others who have reached a mature and beautiful relationship state that it was that very element of lifelong commitment that helped them over the rougher spots of life. Because they were determined to be true to their word, and because they considered their promise a sacred trust, they did not give up when they were tempted to do so. And they are so thankful that they stayed with it.

What they learned in resolving their difficulties proved to be some of the greatest lessons in all their life. Because of their struggle they reached a new level of maturity and fulfillment together.

In lessening the marriage commitment, two people are really programming themselves for defeat. If you think you may not make it, you probably won't. If you open the door to the possibility of failure, you probably will fail. Lowered standards mean lowered attainments. You are satisfied with lesser achievements.

But God did not design human beings for low standards and low achievements. Nor did He design marriage for attaining a reasonable level of happiness and fulfillment. God has given us all unbelievable potential—as individuals and as families. Anything less than the concept of lifelong love and faithfulness just would not be compatible with our God-given potential. And anything less than the earnest desire and true commitment to achieve a rich and satisfying lifelong togetherness would be unworthy of your love and marriage.

Your willingness to stand hand in hand and promise to and with each other, "We will!"—knowing all that is involved and implied in that promise—has gotten you off to a good start. So has your willingness to pattern your life together after God's Scriptural guidelines.

Thank God for those guidelines. Don't look on them as legalistic straitjackets. God did not make people to conform to preconceived rules. He developed the rules of the game afterwards, to help people achieve the greatest and happiest fulfillment in life. And that holds just as true with the directives for marriage as with everything else in His Word.

In Genesis 2:18, 21-25; Matthew 19:1-9; Ephesians 5:21-33; and many other passages, God gives valuable insights into marriage and the roles of husband and wife. Read, study, and pray through them once again. But don't read them with a "We should!" attitude. That usually implies complying without having your heart fully in it.

God describes how beautiful marriage can be. To settle for anything less just isn't good enough. Any response less than an enthusiastic and determined "We will!" is inappropriate.

One thing you must bear in mind is that a "We will!" commitment is an attitude and a mindset. A good marriage, just like anything else that is good, does not happen by chance. There is nothing accidental or lucky about it.

Good marriages are made. They are the result of a lot of hard work coupled with patience and a lot of forgiving love. They are the result of two people consistently joining forces to overcome weaknesses from within and attacks that threaten to erode from without.

You can ask almost anyone what it takes to make a good marriage. With few exceptions they have all the answers. They know what is right and what will strengthen and uphold a healthy relationship. But knowing isn't enough. Without the determination to commit themselves fully to those right answers, they don't stand a chance.

It is not ignorance that tears families apart. A husband and wife will achieve a good marriage only if they are both filled with the desire and the determination to make it good. They need to learn the art of a giving love, a sacrificing love.

That is the love demonstrated by Jesus Christ, who was not only willing but also determined to give His all for our eternal good. His living and dying for us was neither accidental nor a spur-of-the-moment decision. His whole life was designed to meet our human need. Estranged from God by sin, we needed to be reconciled. Christ came to be the Savior, the Reconciler. He came, lived, and died to open the door to unending life and blessing for us. That was His mind-set.

Knowing and accepting Christ and His love are important to us as individuals. They are also important in marriage. In fact, oneness with Christ and oneness in Christ are really central and essential in a good marriage relationship. That oneness puts you on the right track of following the perfect pattern and enables you to understand that love is more than a feeling. Love is a way of life. Love is a course of action.

"Be imitators of God, therefore, as dear children and live a life of love, just as Christ loved us and gave himself up for us" (Eph. 5:1-2). Love as Christ has loved. Forgive as Christ has forgiven. Give as Christ has given. Be compassionate as Christ was compassionate.

There is no more perfect pattern to follow. In all that is necessary for making and maintaining a good and healthy marriage bond, you need only walk in the footsteps of the Savior. He has shown the way.

What's more, we have the divine assurance that we don't have to make it on our own. "Surely I will be with you always," Jesus reminds us (Matt. 28:20). We can turn to Him for help at any time. There's nothing He cannot handle. "Ask and it will be given to you," He promises (Matt. 7:7). "Whatever you ask for in prayer, believe that you have received it, and it will be yours" (Mark 11:24).

Nobody's perfect. Nobody has all the answers. That's one of the first things a Christian learns.

But he also learns that he does not have to be perfect. He does not have to have all the answers, because we have a Lord who is able to supply much more than we even ask or imagine (Eph. 3:20).

Because of that assurance and because of God's faithfulness and dependability, we can be bold enough to say "We will!" and to pledge lifelong love and faithfulness in marriage.

We need the sincere determination. God can make it happen!

Chapter 4

"WE CAN!"

We do!" Together you made the promise to each other.

"We will!" Together you were and are determined to make a good marriage. That's a very good start.

But the question now is, can you?

Of course you can!

Don't be frightened at the negative statistics you hear over and over again—that today there is one divorce for every two marriages. There is a better way of looking at that figure.

Half of the people who become one in marriage make a success of it—actually, more than that. For the one out of two divorce ratio does not show how many are going into a second and third divorce. Failure tends to repeat itself. Far more than half øf today's married couples are making their togetherness work, not just for a few years but on a lifelong basis.

On the other hand, don't be naive about such statistics either. The fact that the majority of people are keeping their marital commitment through their entire life does not necessarily mean that they all have good marriages. Far too many are preserving a shell of a marriage that is less than fulfilling.

Why? "For the sake of the children." "Because we can't afford to get separated." "Because it is against my religion."

They are maintaining an unsatisfactory status quo. They are doing the right thing for the wrong reasons. It's really sad! They still have the potential to make their marriage grow and blossom. But they no longer work at it.

You know people who have succumbed to problems and who live an empty marriage. You can empathize with them. But don't let them condition your thinking about your marriage, or marriage in general.

People have a way of doing that, you know. We really do have tremendous influence on one another—for bad or for good.

Al Capp, in "Li'l Abner," portrayed one little character—Joe with an unpronounceable last name—as a man who was always under a cloud. Though the sun shone brightly everywhere else, it was always raining on his parade. Everywhere he went, he brought gloom. Some people are like that. Their negative feelings and attitudes are really contagious. People who are uptight about their marriages are some of the worst.

Nobody ever said that marriage would transport you to Cloud Nine and that from then on you would float blissfully together on wings of love. You find out soon enough that your feet are still planted on earth, which has its weeds as well as its flowers.

Though you are together, you still continue to experience days of warm sunshine and days of stormy clouds. Sometimes you do not know which is actually better. You begin to recognize that there are mixed blessings in both. Even as you can get burned in the sun, you can be refreshed by a heavy rain. God provides both to nourish life and make it thrive.

It is the way that you accept and use God's daily blessings that will make a difference in your personal and married life.

There is every reason for you to feel absolutely convinced that you can and will have an enriching and fulfilling marriage through all the years ahead. But it's not a matter of self-confidence. That has its way of crumbling when you need it most. It's more than determination. It takes far more than willpower.

It's not that you have been blessed with an extraordinary amount of good common sense and good training to back it up.

It's not because you know that your love is pure and true and that "love conquers all."

If you were to ask people whose marriages ended up in a shambles, you would find that most of them felt they had all of the above. They were determined to make a good marriage. They were sure they could do it. They were passionately in love with each other. They felt they knew all the answers on how to keep their love alive.

If that is the case, why should you—or any of us—feel confident that "We can!" make it? Why be confident that your marriage can meet your fullest expectations and be a source of unending joy and fulfillment?

Because you have one thing going for you that many others do not. You know God!

You know God and have accepted Him as the Creator and Designer of all things. Life owes its existence to Him. Marriage owes its existence to Him. You've learned something of His purpose behind both. And you are willing to follow His way. In fact, you realize there is no better way. What's more, you have come to know God as your Father. You know that His love, which provides for you daily, will also guide you over any rough spots that may lie ahead.

Moreover, you have come to know Jesus and His love. You have accepted Him as your Lord and Savior. You came to realize how empty and lost life is without His love. In Him you found out how to handle your burdens of sin and guilt. You just turned them over to Him, aware that He has already handled them for you. You found in Him not just the pattern but also the power for a beautiful life together. You have the same conviction as Paul: "I can do everything through him who gives me strength" (Phil. 4:13).

You also know that God's Spirit lives in you. The very fact that you have faith is evidence of that. You have been nurturing that faith and that new life in Christ with the special means of nutrition that God has provided for you—His Word and the Lord's Supper. As a child of God, baptized in His name, you have been actively exercising your faith. You worship, you pray, you dig deeply into the Word. You kneel frequently at the altar to receive His body and blood as the assurance of your complete forgiveness and new life.

You do not hesitate to say "We can!" in marriage because you know that God will continue to fill your lives with those special gifts that are so necessary for any human relationship—gifts that are vital in marriage.

"The fruit of the Spirit is love, joy, peace, patience, kindness, goodness, faithfulness, gentleness and self-control." This is the way of life described by Paul as "keeping in step with the Spirit." This is the natural result of being spiritually alive, of "living by the Spirit" (Gal. 5:22-23, 25).

Because of your spiritual walk with God, your new life in Christ, you are able to say confidently, "We can!" Your confidence is not in yourselves. It is in God.

Alone you would still stumble and fall. But as you faithfully follow God's direction and as you implicitly trust Him to provide His power and blessing, you will not fail.

Of course, that does not mean that now it is all up to God, that you can ignore all rules of common sense and the proven paths that lead to happiness and simply trust that the Lord will turn it all to good anyway.

There are certain traits or elements of character that are basic to any good relationship. You need to recognize them and to understand why and how they contribute to the union. You need to develop them.

Working together does not only mean sharing burdens and applying joint effort to common tasks. It also means developing your own selves—trying to be the best person you can possibly become.

This is a good time to take a look at a number of personal character traits. It is also a good time to measure yourself by these standards and to see where there is need for growth and change. Measure YOURSELF. If you also want to measure your partner, do it with the agreement that you will then be willing to sit down and discuss it openly with each other.

If you evaluate only your spouse, you are accomplishing nothing. In fact, you will only be building up feelings that may later vent themselves in the wrong way. But if you will share your appraisal and expose yourself to the same careful analysis, you can help each other in a positive way to develop your true potentials and to make your marriage more mature.

*L*ove is number one. Actually, love is all. In a broad sense love embraces all of the elements that are so necessary for a happy home life.

In "What's Happening to American Families?" (*Better Homes and Gardens*, July 1983) the managing editor quotes an unnamed respondent: "Too many people believe love is just a feeling. If they don't FEEL love for their partner, then they must not love them anymore. This simply is not true. Love is commitment, love is action, love is sacrifice. The feeling is part but it is not the whole."

Paul in 1 Corinthians 13 goes into the practical details of love. It is well worth the time to read this entire chapter together month after month and to discuss its applications for your life.

Paul begins by emphasizing the importance of love. There is no substitute for love. No amount of knowledge or understanding can make up for the absence of love. Faith without love is dead. It really is not faith in the Scriptural sense of the word. Acts of charity and sacrifice are worthless unless they are motivated by true love.

He concludes that love shall outlive and outlast all else. Everything else, including other choice gifts of God, is incomplete and has a limited life-span in God's plan of eternity. But not love.

The greatest gift of all is love—greater even than faith and hope, which will no longer be necessary when we and all the redeemed are in the full presence of God. Then we shall see what until now we have believed on the basis of God's Word and promises. Then we shall enjoy the fulfillment of what so far has been something we can only anticipate.

But love continues beyond time. And when we are with God, we shall love Him all the more. For we shall understand and appreciate Him as we were never able to before. Love is everlasting as God is everlasting, and we also, by His grace and Christ's atoning sacrifice, shall live and love forever.

*L*ove is the greatest. When Jesus was asked about the most important commandment of all, He summed them all up in one word—*love*. What does God expect of us? Love—to love Him with all our heart and soul and mind and strength, and to love our neighbor as ourself.

Nobody takes better care of us than we do ourselves. When we are hungry, we eat. When we are cold, we put on extra clothing. When we feel ill, we take off from work and go to bed. When the illness gets out of hand, we get the best medical help we can. When we are bored, we pay whatever price is necessary to get turned on and tuned in again.

That's exactly how love should work itself out in our relationships with others. And as the old

adage says, charity begins at home. If there is anyone who should be the prime recipient and ben-
eficiary of that kind of love, it is your spouse. No
one should mean more to you. No one should be
treated better by you—more kindly, more consid-
erately—than your spouse. Even though love may
not be limited to the home—and it certainly should
not be—that's where it should be evident in its
greatest warmth and beauty.

In marriage love must be very patient. You know
that neither of you is a perfect or sinless human
being. You both make mistakes. You even repeat
mistakes. You disappoint each other. You fail to
meet each other's expectations. How prone you are
to detect each other's mistakes, and how tempted
you are to point them out. How often you have
yielded to that temptation and harshly criticized,
even nagged, each other.

But that's not the way of love. Love is patient.
In love you bear with one another and help
each other to overcome those mistakes and
disappointments.

Love is forgiving. It certainly is with God. Were
it not, He would have impatiently given up
on us all long ago. Instead He sent His Son to take
our place, to clean our slates, to remove the wrongs
that condemn and consume us.

Forgiving love is rather costly to the forgiver.
There's a big difference between forgiving and sim-

ply tolerating. A person can tolerate without loving. To tolerate means to put up with something, even though you may hate both the deed and the doer.

Forgiving means loving the doer in spite of the deed. It means a willingness to pay whatever price is necessary to undo the harm of what the one you love has done. It means not holding anything against that person, not bringing it up again at some later date as fuel for a new fire that has been sparked.

Of course, there's a companion piece to forgiving love. That is the readiness also to seek and accept forgiveness.

Forgiveness means nothing to the person who senses no need to be forgiven. If someone goes through life self-righteously, belittling the heartache he or she has caused others, it's a different ball game. Love cannot have full sway until there is a change of heart, until one actually seeks to be forgiven.

Forgiving love is also stymied when a person has difficulty in accepting forgiveness. It's hard to love someone who is convinced that he or she does not deserve your love. There are no outer limits to love or forgiveness. Only we can deprive ourselves of these blessings.

The person who cannot accept such forgiving love has problems. It doesn't matter whether it is due to pride or self-condemnation. That marriage is in trouble and will remain in trouble until some help—whether from a pastor, counselor, or friend—can transform those devastating delusions into the positive assurances that are rooted in God's Word and love.

*L*ove requires understanding. Everyone feels the need of being loved. But everyone also has other deep-seated feelings.

Our feelings are conditioned by the events of our daily lives and by our contacts with other people—or lack of them. Because we are individual beings, each different from the other, we differ also in our emotional makeup and in our deep inner personal needs.

You invited friends over to dinner. You went to a great deal of trouble to make sure that everything would be just right. But they never came. At first you charitably chalked it up to unavoidable delay. Then you learned that they had another invitation and just failed to let you know. The husband is angry. He wants to externalize his anger by really telling them off. The wife is hurt. She internalizes by wanting to withdraw and avoid confronting them again.

She hates her husband's temper. He is irritated at her complacency. Both need to understand each other's feelings and to make allowances for them. They cannot let life's irritations create abrasions in the home.

He had a rough day at work. All day long he was sparring and tussling with people who have conflicting interests. After fighting freeway traffic all the way home, all he can think of is a warm meal, a relaxing bath, a little peace and quiet. She was home all day. Though she was perpetually busy, performing one monotonous routine after another, she is bored beyond words. She can hardly wait for him to get home so they can get out and do a few things together.

That's a pretty good stage for some caustic comments and hurt feelings. But that's the way life is—almost every day. How can you maintain an atmosphere of love under such circumstances?

Well, you can. But love requires understanding. And you will never reach understanding without honest and open communication. You must maintain the practice of opening your hearts—and your minds—to each other. Whether you agree with each other or not is not as important as giving each other the opportunity to understand.

*L*ove also means acceptance. That means respecting one another for what each is.

There's a horrible old joke—if it deserves to be called a joke at all—that says the three basic components of a wedding are: aisle, altar, hymn. But as the bride enters the church, those same three words are spelled in her mind: "I'll alter him!"

That's not a good premise for any marriage. There is room in everyone for growth and development. A popular slogan today says: "Be patient.

God isn't finished with me yet." That's true. All through life we make allowances for that. None of us has totally arrived. If we felt we had, we would stagnate. All the challenge and zest would be gone.

In marriage both husband and wife need to encourage each other to such healthy growth. By working together at it, you can both capitalize on the unlimited potential God has given us all.

That is not manipulation. Manipulating is done behind the other's back, against the other's will. Despite noble intentions, manipulating robs a person of self-respect. With the loss of self-respect goes respect for each other.

Appreciate each other for what you really are. God has made each of you a very special jewel. You have your own special worth. Accept that, enjoy it, and make the most of it. You can improve each other. You can facet and polish a diamond. But don't belittle it because it is not an emerald.

*L*ove requires trust. In marriage two people need to have complete confidence in each other. They need to know they can rely and depend on each other.

This of course requires high fidelity in marriage. You understand each other so much, and your love is so true, that you know, no matter what problem or temptation may arise, that each other's response will be proper.

That's a cut above giving the benefit of the doubt. Real trust does not even entertain doubts. When one comes home very late from a meeting, you may worry about whether or not something may have happened on the road. But you don't entertain doubts or suspicions. You know there is a valid reason.

Of course, to complete the picture, it is necessary to remind yourself that trust is built on trustworthiness. Trustworthiness is also love in action. Trust is only the response, the reaction. The two go together. They are inseparable.

*L*ove expresses itself in gentleness, kindness, and considerateness. Love is really tuned in to the feelings of the one you love.

This is part of the growing away from self-centeredness. When the big "I" predominates, when you're turned in on yourself, the needs and feelings of others, even those closest to you, are a secondary consideration. Even the common courtesies are frequently lacking.

Do you sometimes find yourself in the realm of what so many people consider the "little things in life"? They are not the major issues or problems that could spell either victory or defeat, not the threatening storms that could wash away dreams and hopes—just little things—thoughtlessness.

You may persist in doing something even though you know full well that it annoys your spouse. You may fail to recognize the little things you could do to relieve the other of a lot of pressure. You may not even think of the little gestures that tell how much you mean to each other.

Yet these inconspicuous and often unrecognized "little things" are very much like termites. Invisibly they eat away at the basic materials that give strength to a marriage and home. The very fact that they are so small and invisible makes them all the more serious. They can pretty well destroy the whole basic framework and still not be recognized for their destructive nature.

This situation calls for honest examination and preventive maintenance. It's hard to do because it is unsettling and seems threatening. It really pricks the old ego. But it is necessary that couples consciously strive to make "kindness, gentleness, self-control" their standard and habitual way of life.

*L*ove requires maturity.

Several phrases in the Love Chapter (1 Corinthians 13) emphasize this. Love "is not rude, it is not self-seeking, it is not easily angered, it keeps no record of wrongs" (1 Cor. 13:5).

Sometimes we think of the love of a little child as being the purest kind of love in the world. In a sense it is. There is no dishonesty or pretense in it. There are few things than can make you feel so good inside as when a little child comes running to you with sparkling eyes, gives you a big hug and kiss, and then snuggles in. You know you are loved.

Yet there is an imperfectness in the love of a child. It becomes very apparent—and very aggravating—the minute he does not have his way or she does not get what she wants. As beautiful as the love of a child may be, there is a lot of childish selfishness to mar it.

Your marriage improves and matures as your love matures. Maturing means growing out of wanting your own way. Maturity also means rising above touchiness.

It's one thing to expect others to be gentle and considerate to you. But it's another to be overly sensitive. You can't go through life with your "crazy bone" protruding, being hurt and taking offense at everything others do and say. Thin skins create just as many problems in a marriage and home as thick heads.

Immaturity has a way of making mountains out of molehills, rehearsing past grievances, avoiding dealing with problems and issues head-on. Immaturity does not permit a proper perspective. It blows things all out of proportion.

Don't expect to be babied all your life. Grow up, or your love will never reach its potential. Grow up, or you will never receive a healthy love in return.

A mature love is generally marked by a good sense of humor—mature humor, that is, not childish pranks and sick jokes. It is the ability to see through a situation and to realize that it may not be as serious as it might seem initially.

There are certainly times when it is necessary to cry together, but thank God if you can then lift each other's spirits with a smile. The ability to smile in the time of trouble does not mean that a person is naive, does not want to face up to the facts, or does not take anything seriously. It can be a reminder that every problem has a solution. You may not know that solution at the time, but you know that with God's help you will find it. If not, God will have something else, probably even better, in store for you.

Anyway, you're not going to find any answers with your head in your hands, feeling sorry for yourself. Tears blur vision.

Look up in faith. A good sense of humor can contribute greatly to that. With head held high, with a smile on your face and a song in your heart, you can face up to anything. You can find the vein of gold even in the darkest mine.

Right in line with this is a positive spirit. Love that has the ability to act and react positively at all times and under all circumstances is also a special blessing in any marriage and home.

Whether or not a positive spirit makes much sense depends on how close a relationship you have with God. Without true faith, a positive spirit may be little more than whistling in the dark. It may be only blind optimism, wishful thinking.

But for the Christian a positive spirit should be second nature. It is a confession that all is in God's hands and that in God's hands all is well. A Christian can find the positive even in the negative.

Our attitudes and the way we express them set the tone in the marriage. They create the atmosphere in the home. It will be either bright and cheery or gloomy and oppressive. Life and growth depend on light. Darkness only stifles.

As Christians you have the ability to set the right tone, to create the right atmosphere, to make your life together a joyous celebration day after day. You have so much to be thankful for. God has given you so much in each other. Really, how can you have anything less than a bright and positive spirit?

Some of us live in parts of the country where we enjoy sunshine and warmth most of the year. When we visit colder climates, someone will inevitably ask, "Did you bring this good weather with you?"

Wouldn't it be great if you could look at each other and say—and mean—"Darling, you brought this sunshine and warmth with you. You have created a bright and cheery atmosphere in our togetherness. I thank you! And I thank God for you!"

There's no reason it should not be that way in your home—not if you have faith and love and a positive spirit to match.

As you can see, there are many character traits, many elements of personality that make for a happy and blessed marriage. They are all the building blocks, the parts, the components necessary to put the home and family together properly. Please note that they are not like the blocks with which little children play. They are more like the pieces of a jigsaw puzzle. They fit together. They interlock. Not one of them is significant alone. It's when all these pieces fit together that the beautiful picture develops. And so long as any of these pieces is missing, the picture is incomplete. Its full beauty has not yet been reached.

Today's technology provides us with an even better illustration. All the components in a computer system are essential to one another. First of all, a computer must have a central processing unit (CPU). But the CPU really does not do anything by itself. It only enables all the other components to carry out their roles. The keyboard, the screen, the memory bank, be it hard or floppy disk, the printer, the connecting cables—all have specialized functions. Individually and separately they accomplish little. Apart from the CPU they accomplish nothing. What's more, all together, including the CPU, are an assemblage of dead equipment. They can do nothing unless they are plugged into the proper source of power.

In our human relationships, especially in marriage, love is and ever shall be the central processing unit. All the other traits and elements that mean so much in marriage are hollow and lifeless unless they are "driven," given power and life, by love.

But there must be something even beyond that. Our love must be given life and power by the Source of all love and life, God Himself. As Jesus reminds us, we are in a vine-and-branches relationship with Him. As we are one in Him, His life flows through us, and we can bear much fruit. "Apart from me you can do nothing" (John 15:5).

In the final analysis, the love that commits, the love that gives, the love that sacrifices—the love that enables all these other good things so essential to marriage—is not merely learned from Him. It is given by Him.

Chapter 5

WE-
BUILDERS

W e do!" That was the promise and commitment.

"We will!" That is the determination to keep that promise and commitment holy and unbroken until death.

"We can!" Therein lies the confidence that, trusting in God to supply the necessary love and power, the marriage will be blessed through the years.

But so far attention has been directed only to what marriage is and can be and to those particular traits and attitudes that play such a vital role in establishing and maintaining a good and satisfying relationship.

Obviously there is more to it than that. What about the daily living? How do you handle the stresses and tensions that inevitably arise? How do you cope with the problems that crop up so frequently? What is the best way to resolve the differences and difficulties we tend to make for ourselves?

You learn soon enough that there are no secret ingredients. There is no magic formula.

On the other hand, there are certain deliberate courses of action that strengthen marriage and keep love alive. But here again, knowing them is not enough. They are courses of action. It is necessary to work at the action required—and to work at it together.

Let's call such courses of action "We-Builders" and explore a few of them together.

An extremely important "We-Builder" is to acknowledge, agree on, accept, and appreciate the role that each of you has assumed in your marriage.

Can you imagine a Broadway play in which none of the actors or actresses are sure of which part they are playing or which lines are theirs? Even what is called "improvisation" has certain basic understandings and agreements established beforehand.

The playwright envisions the theme or story line, developes the script, fleshes out the characters, and, together with the director, selects who is best suited to each role. But even after this has been completed, it is not yet time for the curtain to go up.

The actors must think themselves into their parts. They study and prepare. Like bride and groom, they get opening night jitters. But at least they are ready. They know who they are and what is expected of them.

Marriage is not playacting. It is meant for the long run, not the short season. In marriage it is doubly important to know who you are and what is expected of you. How do your roles interrelate? How can you support and enhance rather than up-stage each other?

Many people seem to go at marriage as if it were improvisational theater. Though there are a few accepted givens, life is pretty much ad-libbed. There's a general understanding to play it as it comes. The production is one unending succession of reactions. There's no planning. If it goes any-where, it is more accidental than intentional. Often it falls flat. Even the most talented, alert "improv group" admits that you can stay fresh only so long. It may be fun for a while, but you soon want to move on into something more substantial. It may be a good way to test your abilities. But you soon want to apply those abilities to something lasting.

Marriage and married life do not have to be improvised. The same God who made us all—the God who designed marriage as the prime human relationship—has also developed the script. He has given us detailed descriptions of the roles the part-ners in marriage will play. Best of all, He did not draw up His cast of characters and then begin a search to see if anyone could conceivably fill those roles. First He designed us. Then He designed the roles to match us, not vice versa.

Summary statements on these roles are found in Scripture, most fully in Ephesians 5. Though those verses do offer pointed counsel to husbands and wives individually, it should be noted that they are introduced with a number of principles that apply equally to both.

Space does not permit extensive comments, elaboration, or interpretation of these principles. Nor are they needed.

> Be imitators of God . . . and live a life of love, just as Christ loved us and gave himself up for us as a fragrant offering and sacrifice to God (vv. 1-2).
>
> Among you there must not be even a hint of sexual immorality, or of any kind of impurity, or of greed, because these are improper for God's holy people (v. 3).
>
> You are light in the Lord. Live as children of light (v. 8). . . . Have nothing to do with the fruitless deeds of darkness" (v. 11).
>
> Be very careful, then, how you live—not as unwise but as wise, making the most of every opportunity (vv. 15-16). . . . Be filled with the Spirit. Speak to one another with psalms, hymns and spiritual songs. Sing . . . in your heart to the Lord, always giving thanks to God the Father for everything, in the name of our Lord Jesus Christ" (vv. 18-20).
>
> Submit to one another out of reverence for Christ (v. 21).

In that context the special directives to husbands and wives follow immediately. First they are addressed to the wife:

> Wives, submit to your husbands (v. 22).

This is not a new subject. It is an extension of what has just been said, that as Christians we

submit ourselves to one another out of reverence
for God. Where is it more natural for such submitting and serving one another in love to begin
than in the home, in the marital relationship?

> Wives, submit to your husbands as to the Lord
> (v. 22).

What's this? Has a new Lord been established?
Not at all!

The wife should rather recognize that in marriage her beloved husband has assumed a new and
heavy responsibility—that is, if he actually accepts
His God-given role. For what God is asking of him
is that he live a totally self-sacrificing love for his
wife. In so doing he is motivating the same kind of
love and respect from her that we have for our
Lord.

> Husbands, love your wives, just as Christ loved
> the church and gave himself up for her (v. 25).

Why did Christ give Himself? Love. His heroic,
sacrificial, and victorious life and death were not a
macho demonstration of the power of God. It was
His infinite concern for us all that moved Him to
pay so great a price. He did it to remove everything
that could keep us from becoming the perfect kind
of people God envisioned in the first place. He did
it to remove everything that might prevent us from
receiving and enjoying the full and eternal blessings of heaven. He did it to save His body of believers.

Now we are bound to Him as one body. In faith we see Him as our Head. We honor Him, we worship Him, we respect Him as our Lord and Head, and we gladly submit our wills to His in an earnest desire to serve Him. For even the greatest service we render fades into insignificance in the light of the much greater love and service He has first shown to us.

What if Jesus had not done it? What if He had shirked the responsibility that love laid on Him? That's a ridiculous premise. The point is, He did what He came to do. And because He did, we submit ourselves to Him in love and in the fear of God.

What about the husband? His role is clearly spelled out. His love for his wife is to be a committing love—like Christ's. It is to be a giving love—like Christ's. It is to be a sacrificing love— like Christ's. It is a role of loving another above self.

> Each one of you also must love his wife as he loves himself, and the wife must respect her husband (v. 33).

In the light of the above, it's hard to even imagine anyone suggesting that the statement about "submitting" smacks of subservience—or male chauvinism. Submitting is a natural expression of what we feel, of our appreciation and respect for what has been done for us. God has constructed a two-way street of love and mutual service.

What if the husband doesn't assume his role as outlined? Does that then change the role of wife? Frankly, both questions are out of order. The pattern has been presented. Blessing lies in our trying to come up to the ideal, not in trying to devise an alternate second best.

By the way, note that the role descriptions do not go beyond these broad basics of serving one another in love.

They do not say that the man must be the sole support or primary breadwinner or that a wife must be chief cook and housekeeper. Traditional as these roles may be, they are neither sacred nor inviolate.

It's true that certain things may be more natural, better suited to one than the other. That's how traditions are born. Since the man has a more muscular frame and is not subject to periods of pregnancy and childbirth, it is understandable that it would fall on him primarily to provide financial stability and security for his wife and children. But what if he becomes ill or handicapped? What if hard times fall on him, and he encounters periods of unemployment?

As a mother, it is inevitable that the role of the wife centers more around family and home. No one is more suited or better equipped physically and emotionally for such responsibility. It's hard to find an adequate substitute for her special kind of love and care.

But she also has special skills and abilities, goals and objectives that she was trained to achieve. She also has needs to be fulfilled and a call to use her time and God-given talents productively. She may gladly forego them, devoting herself totally to her marriage and family during those critical years of childbearing and child training. But must she give them up entirely? Is it wise? Is it necessary?

Her special talents may make her a potentially better breadwinner than her husband. Is that wrong? Should he feel put down or threatened by that? He may find that nothing relaxes him more or gives him more enjoyment than to work in the kitchen and imagine himself a gourmet chef. Is that unmasculine? Is he invading her territory? What if they agree that he is a better cook and that the quality of both of their lives, as well as that of the rest of the family, is improved by a few trade-offs in roles?

There certainly are no major principles involved, Scriptural or otherwise. Pride may get in the way, but it does not have to. The basic principles remain unchanged—submitting to one another in love and respect and working together to make as strong and good a home as possible in line with the directives of God's Word.

What matters above all is that they are agreed, that they make decisions together after much praying and discussing, and that there be no confusion or misunderstanding as to who is assuming what responsibility and why.

One thing more: Even if there is perfect agreement and harmony in the decisions made, and even if everything is working out to their best advantage, they had better steel themselves against the negative opinions, catty remarks, and caustic criticisms of "friends" who feel that the rules of the game of life call for inflexible stereotypes. But then, that's their problem, not yours! Right?

A second "We-Builder" follows closely on the agreement on roles. The prophet Amos asked long ago: "Do two walk together unless they have agreed to do so?" (3:3).

In agreeing on roles, especially if they vary from more commonly accepted patterns, it is essential to know and agree on your goals and objectives.

Where are you going? Do you know how to get there? Do you know what it will cost in terms of money and personal effort? Are you willing to pay that price? What contribution will each of you be making in order to reach that goal?

Every couple finds sooner or later—usually sooner—that just being married is not enough. A good marriage requires a game plan, a well-thought-out strategy. All too often families find themselves with a profusion of unrelated game plans—his, hers, and eventually also the children's.

The result is tension and conflict. They realize that they are at cross-purposes, working against each other. If the situation is unresolved, there is unhappiness, a drawing away from one another, and perhaps even bitterness.

There's really only one way to avoid this. That is sitting down together at the very beginning, and frequently ever after, to see how the various elements of their personal lives can be fitted together for the good of their marriage and family.

At times this can be quite difficult. We all tend to develop certain "sacred cows." We feel threatened if anyone even dares to question them.

A person's work can easily become a sacred cow. There is an insatiable drive to reach the top. The rest of the family just has to understand and make the necessary sacrifices.

But do they? How does this drive contribute to the family good? Only financially? Is that really enough? How does it fit in with the total long-range plan?

Maybe it does fit in. As the family prays and discusses it together, they may conclude that it is worth it and that they can adjust—at least for a while. But for how long? When and where are the checkpoints so progress or lack of progress can be measured?

Maybe it does not fit in. Sometimes a person just has to face up to the fact that he or she is in a work situation that will never be anything less than all-consuming. Like the sacred cows in India that roam unmolested, eating food that may be needed by the starving masses and providing no source of food in themselves, one's work or profession may not really be delivering the goods. It may actually deprive the family of what it promised to provide.

What then? As hard as it may be, it's time for a change. A person's work is to make it possible for the family to eat, not to be eaten. The earth is littered with the wreckage of too many families who hung in there just because the impossible job continued to offer illusions of more money, higher social position, top executive status, and the feeling of importance. But, as Jesus asked: "What good is it for a man to gain the whole world, yet forfeit his soul?" (Mark 8:36)—or his family or marriage?

It is also imperative that no one build fences around what he or she considers his or her "own business." Any such ploy shuts out the others from an important phase of life. Rather pray and discuss everything to the point of agreeing together on what would be most appropriate.

That holds true of everything that pertains to the common goals and objectives in a home. Money management is a big one. Plan together for major expenditures and a savings plan. Put together a budget that will make it possible to attain these ends and then hold to that budget.

The key again is having clearly defined goals and working together towards them. That's a real "We-Builder."

A third is for you both to look on your marriage as a career. One thing about a career is that you really work at it. You don't advance very far if you take a casual attitude towards it. You give it your best.

You seek out growth and enrichment programs. You constantly try to sharpen your talents and improve your abilities. You stretch your horizons and establish new and more challenging goals. You make personal sacrifices to attain them.

People who have had successful careers all tell the same story—it takes a little bit of luck, but a lot of hard work.

Treat your marriage the same way you would a career. Make it your career—your first and foremost career. Keep up the learning process to keep up the growing process. Don't overlook marriage enrichment programs, which give you an opportunity to learn some of the ways in which others have strengthened their marriages. Maybe you will not learn a thing you did not already know. But it can encourage you by showing that you are on the right path. And it can reassure you that it is worth all the hard work you are putting into it together. And it can help and encourage others, who are struggling to achieve a marriage as good as yours.

Make marriage your first career? Is there any other that pays you the same kind of lifelong benefits?

Another "We-Builder" is making time for each other.

There is no doubt about it, we are living in the fast lane. It seems we never have enough time to do all the things we want to do, not even all the things we should be doing. Something has to be cut back. Unfortunately, too often we cut short the time that is badly needed in our marriage and home.

Understandably, the greater portion—and the better portion—of the day is spent at work and in commuting to and from work. Occasionally work makes demands for additional time. We seldom have control over that.

In our desire to grow, we enroll in educational programs, which require another major chunk of time. Our church is important to us. Worship and Bible study are a high priority. We also feel obligated to teach, to sing in the choir, or to serve on boards and committees. In our community we try to be good citizens and to help in worthy causes. We also need some time to be friendly and helpful to our neighbors.

As children reach school years, another straw is placed on the camel's back. Actually, it is not a straw but a log. PTAs, after-school activities, evening programs, athletic teams and leagues, drill teams, bands, dance lessons, clubs—why go on?

Familywise, you feel as if you have been sprayed out of an atomizer. Home takes on the appearance of a key club. It's become a place where everyone comes at his own convenience for some good food, a little relaxation and entertainment, a shower, and a change of clothes and then leaves.

Editorials properly deplore the loss of the family table. Every effort should be made to have at least one meal in the day in which husband and wife and children sit and eat together. Every family needs true quality family time.

But is the problem really a lack of time? If things get out of hand, is it not because we failed to set proper priorities on our time? Here again it is a matter of sitting down together and developing a mutually agreeable program and schedule. We may not be able to take part in all the worthwhile activities that clamor for our participation. It is no sin to say no.

Besides, just because an activity takes you away from home does not mean it has to deprive you of meaningful togetherness. You can do more together. Your marriage can be strengthened by worshiping together, by taking a course together. Your family life can be enriched by attending a sporting event or program in which your child is participating and then sitting down and talking about it together.

You are sharing interests. But it is important that the interests of all be taken into consideration, not just the interests of one.

On the other hand, spending more time at home together does not necessarily mean enrichment or satisfying fulfillment. It's not how much time you have but what you do with your time that counts.

Being together is not always true together-ness—not even being together in the same room, doing the same thing. That's becoming increasingly apparent with television viewing. Once heralded for bringing and keeping the family together, it is now properly being questioned. Often real togetherness is not achieved until the set has been turned off. Only then is the stage set for talking, for opening hearts and minds to each other. And that's where true togetherness begins.

In that connection, we should all be grateful for video recorders. They are helping many couples make better use of their private times together. Instead of being glued to the TV on Saturdays, Sundays, Monday nights, Thanksgiving, and New Year's Day for the matrimonial nemesis known as football, the husband can now share those choice family days and hours more beneficially without missing the games. Something good is happening!

We-Building" takes place when you make time for each other. That takes deliberate effort. It may also take compromise. Finding time is one thing. Finding the right time may be quite another.

You soon discover in marriage that your mental clocks are not necessarily synchronized with each other. The wife has something troubling her, and she tells her husband that they need to talk. She is disappointed in his "Please, not now!" Now what? Conflict? Argument? Or does she walk away feeling rebuffed?

There are two principles here. One is that he owes it to her to give her the opportunity to share what is on her mind and to help her through this difficulty. The other is that she owes it to him to respect his judgment that this may not be the best time.

What is the resolution? Determine together first how urgent the matter is. Maybe it does require immediate attention. Maybe it could be momentarily delayed, and another early time could be scheduled to discuss it. But here again it is important that the time be arranged and that the set time be kept, as surely as if it were an important business appointment.

Everyone has need for a certain amount of private time and private space. But you can never grow together unless you are together adequately. So make time for each other—enough to meet each other's needs. Making time for each other is a "We-Builder." So is taking time for God.

About one-third of all the families in trouble recognize and admit that one of the contributing factors to their difficulty is the lack of an adequate religious foundation. That's probably true of far more, but many just do not recognize it. As one couple expressed it: "If we had put God first in our lives, we would have had far fewer problems."

"The family that prays together, stays together." You don't hear that adage as much in recent years. It was appropriated by too many others who twisted it to serve their purposes and was quickly followed by dozens of variants.

But the saying is just as truthful and forceful as ever. Togetherness is not complete togetherness unless it includes the spiritual dimension. A vital link is missing when a husband and wife cannot or do not pray or worship together. That same void is apparent—and it certainly gives mixed signals about what is important and unimportant—when parents drop off their children at Sunday school but do not participate in Bible study or worship themselves.

Every marriage and every home needs strong spiritual foundations. The way some go at it, religion serves as little more than a decorative touch— like pictures on walls, lace curtains, or collectors' edition books (never opened or read) to pretty up the shelves. Yet it is the spiritual that is the bedrock, the strong support on which the security of the home and family is dependent.

In a very important way a faith-filled relationship with God is personal. Every person needs time alone with God—time in the Word and time in prayer. Such moments of spiritual refreshment go a long way in helping one through the day.

But time together in the Word and prayer are equally important for husbands and wives, and later also with the children. It's not just the act or habit of a devotional period. Perfunctorily observed, it could prove a waste of time. But when you together approach God with open hearts and open minds, with the determination to hear and learn and to translate that into your daily life, you will be richly blessed.

Unfortunately, there is much room for improvement in family devotions. Churches and publishers try to help by producing usable and sometimes excellent materials. But so many use them in a ritualistic rather than thought-provoking way. So little time is used in follow-up, in discussing and applying the material read. So many prayers are read; so few are offered from the heart. So seldom is the process reversed so that the couple identifies a personal need and then searches the Scriptures together to find God's answers for it. Yet how much more profitable that would be.

Take time for God every day, and do it together. It not only exposes you to God's guidance, but it enables you to sense His presence more fully. You together come to know and appreciate Him ever more. In prayer you draw on His power. You find healing for your hurts and wounds.

In your time with God you gain a new sense of appreciation of yourselves also. You are special people, and God loves you. He never would have sent Jesus to be your Savior had He not felt you were worth saving. When God loves you so much that He did not spare even His Son, you can be sure that out of that same love He watches over you and guards and blesses you at all times.

Make sure that Jesus is central in your marriage and home—not just as a guest, but as an important member of your family. Make sure that you consult Him in all your family decisions.

You will also find yourselves blessed as you make time for God in the company of other Christians. That's not to say that you will necessarily always feel uplifted or helped every time you go to church. Some Sundays God may use your presence primarily as an encouragement to someone else. But the fact that you worshiped shows that you consider God and His will top priority in your life.

More good is effected by the habits of regular home devotions and regular church worship than you may ever know. Brushing your teeth daily can seem like a monotonous and useless routine at times. Nothing seems to be happening. But the absence of decay proves that it has been a healthful and worthwhile habit.

The New Testament describes the church as the body of believers, of which Christ is the Head. All parts differ in appearance and function. Yet as each does his thing, the whole body benefits—including that individual member. In the church, as in the human body, it often happens quite imperceptibly. But it's happening! And God is making it happen!

Like the couple said, "If we had put God first

in our lives, we would have had a lot fewer problems." Make time for God! Do it together!

Another important "We-Builder" is maintaining open lines of communication.

If a husband and wife cannot or do not communicate effectively with each other, they are headed for serious problems. If they cannot or do not share their true thoughts and feelings honestly and openly with each other, their marriage is in trouble. In fact, almost 90 percent of today's divorced couples say that their inability to communicate finally convinced them they could never make it together.

The need of a husband and wife to communicate effectively with each other seems so self-evident. It is such simple common sense that it is hard to believe it could be such a trouble spot in so many marriages.

Where does the difficulty lie? If we think back to an earlier "We-Builder," it could lie in not taking enough time for each other. But it goes much deeper than that.

Actually we take too much for granted in the communication process.

A husband brought his wife a box of candy for her birthday. She thanked him coolly and went about her business. Later that evening he pinned her down. "What's wrong? You're just not yourself." She snapped, "I should have thought that you would know by now that candy is an inappropriate gift. You never give any thought to what I might really like. And besides, I'm on a diet."

The problem? Poor communication—actually, no communication. "I should have thought that you would know by now." Maybe he should have been more attentive to her feelings and likes and dislikes. But she should have been more open in expressing those feelings to him too. Second-guessing is not good communication. It's not fair to expect a spouse to sense what you want or how you feel.

Bad listening habits also contribute to poor communication. We are so beset by so many distractions most of the time that we tend to become preoccupied. What others say flies right by us. We heard the sound and probably even recall some of the words. But our thoughts were never on track.

A school for the deaf in the East made its well-equipped van available to give hearing tests to delegates at a recent midwestern convention. One man came in stating that his wife thought it might be a good idea for him to get his ears checked because his hearing did not seem to be as sharp as it used to be. After all the high level, low level, and volume tests had been completed on each ear, he was surprised to learn that his hearing score had been rated high. The attendant went on to explain that the problem he had was a very common malady. In the profession it was known as "spousal deafness."

"Honey, I told you that this morning!"

"You did not! If you had, I certainly would have remembered."

"I distinctly remember telling you. You were sitting right there reading the paper . . ."

Preoccupation. What's the solution? Is it that the moment the dulcet tones of her voice are heard, he should throw his mental switch, put down the paper, forget everything else he has been thinking about, and give undivided attention to what she is saying? Impossible! The mind does not function that way. He probably was not even conscious that she was speaking to him until she was already past the punch line.

In this case good communication calls for more understanding on her part. Accept the fact that he really is interested in what she is saying. Give him a moment to recognize that he needs to change gears mentally. And then double-check to make sure he really did hear and understand, not in an officious way, as if she is giving a test, but giving him a perfectly normal way to feed back his understanding. Criticism and an officious attitude are put-downs. They tear down self-respect, as does anything else that makes a person feel treated like a child.

Communication problems do not fall exclusively into the domain of marriage. They occur whenever and wherever anyone is trying to convey message and meaning to anyone else. It happens in writing as well as in speaking. No typewriter has yet been invented that has eliminated the possibility of people reading between the lines.

That's why there are dozens of books written on the subject and seminars and college courses on "The Art of Communication." A baby may get by on communicating with little more than a cry or a pout. But as many a harried mother can testify, he isn't really communicating much more than unhappiness. Hers is now the exasperating task of sorting out whether he is hungry, wet, sick, tired, or just plain nasty and disagreeable.

Effective communicating is truly a refined art that needs to be developed, also in the home. As we mature in our relationship, we should be growing also in our ability to express ourselves properly to each other. We should also recognize that despite our best intentions and noblest efforts, misunderstandings may still arise.

Communication may break down at many places along the line. I know what I want to say, but I may not be absolutely clear in my thinking. I may then have difficulty in putting it into the right words. The hearer may have difficulty in following me. The hearer may also have slightly different understandings of some of the words I used or a different perspective so that he may not even sense where I am coming from. So there is nothing unusual, and certainly nothing insensitive or neglectful, if my message is not picked up as I intended it.

That's true even in the home—even with lovers who like to think that they don't need words to communicate!

As close as you may be, what one says may not be what the other hears. She greets him, "You're home later than usual." The chip flies off his shoulder. There she goes again, criticizing me for being late. But what she meant was: "Traffic must have been bad again. I'm sure glad you got home safely!"

When they are dressed to go out to dinner, he likes what he sees and comments, "Is that a new dress?" Now here's one that can open the door to all sorts of communication difficulties. It so happens that it is not a new dress. It has been hanging in the closet unworn for quite some time. Reaction 1: "Doesn't he ever pay any attention to my clothes? You'd think he would have recognized this dress. Goodness knows, I've had it for years." Or reaction 2: "Does he think I go out and buy new clothes every time I turn around? Well, if he thinks it, I might as well go out and do it. Goodness knows, I could use a few new things." Yet her response should have been: "Thank you! It's nice to know you still think I look good."

Explore together this whole process of communicating. Realize that it is equally important to communicate feelings and moods, and to communicate them honestly.

It's a bit unfortunate that we adults try to hide our feelings as much as we do. Life is not a poker game. Winning is not contingent on how completely you can fool others. We need to understand one another, not deceive each other. We want to come out on top together, not alone.

If you are unhappy over something, say so. If something turns you on and makes you feel good, say so. The intimate sharing of your feelings—also in your sexual relations—will do more than anything else to bring about the understanding and closeness so vital to a good marriage.

Get in the habit of opening up to each other. Describe your feelings honestly, whether they are positive or negative. Don't wait until you are ready to explode. Letting off steam will only set up an antagonistic situation. It will put the other on the defensive.

But you can avoid the heat of friction if you open up in a nonabrasive way. If you can share your hurts and anxieties without bitterness or sarcasm, you will strike a responsive note. And you will see again just how helpful and loving and supporting your partner can be.

Keep those lines open. Keep the busy signals and the putting on hold to a minimum. Say what you mean, and mean what you say.

*L*earning to work together is another real "We-Builder."

This goes back again to setting joint goals and objectives—setting the goal, assessing the cost, determining together what contributions in personal effort each can make to reach that goal. It also goes back to your agreed perceptions and understandings of your roles in your marriage. What do you have the right to expect of each other?

But after all the expectations and understandings have been clearly established, there is still the hard work of making it happen. And it is hard work, calling for a lot of love and sacrifice!

The sooner you can get over the "That's not my job!" syndrome, the better off your marriage will be. It's unfortunate that there is such a deeply ingrained mentality that says, The house, especially the kitchen, is her responsibility; the garage and yard are his. Why? Who made those rules?

What's wrong with working out in the yard together? As one mows and the other clips, they are enjoying the sunshine and fresh air together, and the job gets done faster. And what's wrong with doing the dishes together? There are few times more conducive to unhurried conversation.

What's wrong with cleaning the garage or doing housework or painting a room together? There's more true togetherness in any of these than in watching a TV program together. The need for that type of togetherness is all the more apparent when both husband and wife have full-time jobs away from the home. If attaining mutually established goals requires both to work away from the home, then certainly it also means that both must work together within the home too.

There is one potential trouble area though. When the going gets rough and the burden a bit heavy, there is all too often the temptation to begin to compare. In a moment of frustration, one complains, "You're not really holding up your end of the deal," or "You know, you are not really contributing as much as you think you are."

This becomes an arena for argument. It's not too bad—actually, it can be healthy—to argue. To voice differing, even opposing, points of view will provide a fuller and a clearer picture. Both benefit as the dimensions of the problem are more clearly defined. It is then possible to attack the problem more realistically and to solve it.

That kind of arguing and struggling never hurt any marriage. The damage begins when you stop fighting the problem and begin to fight each other.

The new problem then is competition. The new obsession is to become the winner. Working against each other has set in. Everything is judged as a win-or-lose situation.

We grew up flipping coins. "Heads you win, tails you lose." We looked at everything, trying to distinguish the "either" from the "or." It seemed so simple that way.

But life is never that simple. Its issues are far too complex to call for the toss of a coin. Moreover, marriage is one institution that does not benefit from a win-lose situation.

In marriage if one wins, both win. If one loses, both lose.

Marriage must never degenerate into a competitive contest with one person trying to best the other. It must always remain a cooperative togetherness. You may enjoy the competition, even against each other, in the games you play. But marriage and family are not that type of game.

After you are put down so many times, you build up a tremendous resentment against your antagonist. Your self-image has been defaced. You try to protect yourself by keeping your distance. The eventual distance is called divorce.

So when the temptation to fight to win comes, cool it. Think through the consequences. What do you want—a momentary victory or a lasting marriage? That's a good time also to pray for the wisdom and strength to draw your partner into a cooperative solution so that love will not be strained.

Now don't get the idea that there is no room or opportunity for fighting in marriage. There is! Learning to fight together can be another healthy exercise in "We-Building."

When you entered marriage, you knew full well that you would encounter many difficulties along the way. As long as you are in the world and society, you will have to face the ills and evils that everyone else faces. There is no dead bolt you can install that will effectively lock out all tensions and trials.

Scripture warns that there are many evils around us that "war against your soul" (1 Peter

2:11). As you take note of them, you recognize that they also war against a Christian marriage.

Wily Satan does not waste much time on frontal attacks. He knows too well that it is far easier to start a disintegration from within. But he does know how to use adverse outside forces, too.

He doesn't always use a powerful overwhelming force. The old fable of the wind and the sun contains timeless truth. Which was the stronger? A contest was arranged to see who could get the coat off the traveler's back. The wind blew furiously. The more it blew, the colder the traveler became, and the more tightly he wrapped his coat around him. The sun in turn smiled warmly on the man. It only took a few moments before he removed his coat to get relief from the sun's rays.

We all face stormy days at times. Some things are just plain hard to take. You have worked hard and faithfully for the same employer for many years. Suddenly you are advised that the impending cutback will also include you. On top of that, you are informed that your company retirement benefits are nowhere near what you had been led to believe. And all that comes just when you read constantly that the Social Security program is in trouble.

All your life you dreamed of being a teacher. You could not imagine any more satisfying profession. You worked hard for your degree and teaching credential. You taught for a number of years and found it to be as rewarding as you anticipated. So you made the sacrificial plunge. You went back to school for advanced degrees so you could do an even better job of teaching. Your whole family felt the pinch, but you all agreed it would be worth it.

Now you have your doctorate. You apply for another teaching position, only to learn that the schools are cutting back. The expansion brought on by the baby boom is over. Additionally, state funding is running low. Aren't they hiring? Yes, to a small degree. But they want new teachers. They can be paid less. You are overqualified. "But I'd work for less!" you protest. But they still dismiss you lightly, contending that you would never be satisfied working below your potential.

We all encounter our stormy days. Sometimes the clouds roll in so thickly that they totally obliterate the sun. It is hard at times like that to realize that up beyond those clouds the sun is still shining.

You've always enjoyed perfect health. There has seldom been a time when you were not able to carry your full day's work—and then some! Suddenly you find yourself on sick leave. Normal benefits have already been supplanted by disability payments. How much longer will this go on? How long can I be a burden to my loved ones before they get tired of it? How are we going to meet the increased expenses?

Those are stormy days all right. And there are many others like them. But in themselves they really neither disrupt nor destroy a good marriage. Instead you pool your team resources and work and fight together that much harder to overcome the threat.

No, it's the subtler intrusions that prove the most disruptive—like enjoying too much the flirtatious advances of an overfriendly neighbor (had there been a Mrs. Joseph at the time that Joseph served in Potiphar's household, she would have been very proud and appreciative of her husband for the moral integrity he showed) or investing the family savings in a "can't miss" business venture despite the protests that "we don't have money to throw around." The second stage comes slightly later when there is only the paper to show for "what might have been."

These are outside forces too, just like the bigger threatening storms. If we let them, they could easily wedge themselves between husband and wife.

The family really pulls together against the big threats. You realize that in all things God can work "for the good of those who love him" (Rom. 8:28). Despite the seriousness of the storm, your unity is not undermined. Conversely, you learn all the more how to fight and work together. Times like that generally end up as building rather than demolition experiences.

But the little things can really throw you. Watch out for them!

W e-Building" also requires keeping the excitement alive.

One cynic has asked, "Is there truly life after marriage?" He tried it. He didn't like it. He preferred the chase to the trophy, the hunt to the catch. Once married, he felt stifled. The spark was gone.

That really is an indictment of the man rather than of his marriage. The more he described his disappointment, the more it became apparent that he had really put nothing into his marriage. Why should he have expected to get anything out of it?

On the other hand, it pays to listen to a voice like his occasionally. For it is true that too many married couples settle into a rut and never get out of it again.

Before marriage, you used to fight to have time together. Personal schedules and commitments were adjusted frequently so you could spend another evening together. You wracked your brain for some new activity that you could enjoy together. No two dates were alike. You were constantly searching for new ways of surprising and pleasing each other.

Why should it be different after marriage? It shouldn't, but it generally is. It is not marriage that is at fault. We just no longer go to such lengths to keep it alive, fresh, and exciting.

It needn't cost a lot. You don't have to overwhelm each other with expensive gifts. In fact, if the price tag is a major consideration, it can get out of hand pretty quickly. Anyway, you can't measure love by the number of ciphers behind the dollar sign.

It may not cost much at all—in terms of money. But it certainly does take a lot in terms of thought and thoughtfulness. And it should!

Excitement comes when patterns are broken. When the same things happen over and over again—no matter how thoughtful and appropriate they may be—you begin to take them for granted. They take on the aspect of a "no-thought" gift.

You gave her one long-stemmed rose on her birthday. Beautiful! She cherished the memory of it long after the petals were fallen. In fact, those very petals are still pressed between the pages of a favorite book. But to make that *the* birthday ritual for the rest of her life—no other gift, no kind of surprise—gets a little boring, doesn't it?

He likes potato pancakes. Despite the mess, she decided to surprise him by making them Friday evening. He was so happy and enjoyed them so much that now she makes potato pancakes every Friday night.

One of the greatest and most fun-filled adventures in married life is the ongoing hunt for new and fresh activities. Don't let apathy set in. Break the patterns. Don't get bound by slavish routines.

That's the secret of staying fresh on the job too. Vary your activities. About the time that your current activity is proving to be monotonous and boring, put it aside. Switch to something different. You end up being far more productive.

Make it a practice to approach your time together at home in the same way. It becomes boring to get home at 6:00, eat at 6:30, have a brief devotion at 7:00, take a walk at 7:15, turn on television at 8:00, and go to bed at 11:00—night after night.

That's why taking some evening courses together can be a pleasant change—or a Bible study group, dinner at a restaurant with a candle-lit atmosphere, a hobby or sport you can enjoy together, a marriage enrichment program—just so it's not always the same thing.

Do a better job of planning your vacations too. It can be pleasant indeed to get away from home and spend a few weeks in a modest but comfortable cabin on a lakeshore. But should that be your whole vacation every year? Is that life—49 weeks with your nose to the grindstone and then three weeks in the same old place doing the same old thing?

Don't knock it! That may be exactly what is most satisfying to many people. If so, more power to them. But that is setting the stage for a marriage to go stale. It may result more in a mere peaceful coexistence than in a growing, exciting marriage.

God made a whole, wide, wonderful world! There is an endless variety of wonders of nature to observe. Every one of them teaches us something about His love and power, His sense of beauty and orderliness—gentle beaches and craggy bluffs;

green rolling hills and rocky snowcapped mountains; giant redwoods standing on sentinel duty and hardwoods painting fall landscapes with brilliant colors; lazy muddy rivers that serve as highways for boats and barges and cold, clear streams to delight the fisherman; towering, noisy cities with monuments to just about anything and fertile fields with crops to provide sustenance for the teeming masses. It's all there—endless variety just for the taking!

And people—how enriching to get away from our own little familiar circle and observe how others live—city people, farm people, hill and mountain folk, backwoods pioneers, and fisherfolk; northerners, southerners, midwesterners, east- and west-coasters; villages with distinct and differing ethnic and cultural backgrounds and pockets of the same in large cities. There's so much to learn about others—and through them about yourselves.

It doesn't have to stop at the borders of your own country either. Becoming acquainted with the land and the people within is only scratching the surface. There's a whole world out there, with unbelievably exciting diversity.

Neither life nor marriage has to grow stale. They won't as long as you exercise your imagination in seeking out and making new experiences.

It doesn't even have to involve travel or extended periods of time. Spend special days with special people. Just break the routine. And remember that the planning can be almost as much fun as the doing, just as long as you do it together.

One thing more—make your home a life center, not just a living center. Shared usage of rooms and furniture does not make it a life center. Only shared love and united hearts and minds will.

Make your home like the hub of a wheel, where everything is truly together. Though the member spokes may be functioning quite apart from each other where the rubber hits the road, their strength and ability to function lies in their being truly united at the hub.

Home then is not merely a retreat, a hiding place or hermitage where you go to escape and avoid the realities of life. Home is the reality. Your good marriage has made it so. It is where you are constantly regenerated by love, charged up again to meet and handle all that comes.

There are many other things that can be put into the category of "We-Builders." There is no end to the ways that marriage can be strengthened and kept healthily alive.

Yes, there is indeed a lot of conscious thought and effort that goes into making and keeping a good marriage. But it pays off in such rich dividends. It's hard to even imagine anything else so personally rewarding and so constructively satisfying.

But be prepared for a lot of change along the way.

Some people find that a bit unsettling. "It just isn't like it used to be," one after another laments. Well, thank God for that. Change is beneficial. You change. Your needs change. Your interests change. Why shouldn't your marriage change? Change is essential to growth.

In your first years of marriage your prime need and desire is to get really close to one another. You are settling in together from two different backgrounds. You are anxious to know everything possible about each other, to achieve a high level of intimacy. You are caught up in the exciting rapture of love. You never knew that any kind of relationship could be this wonderful. More than anything else, you want to be with and please each other.

The next stage is both similar and different. With intimacy established you now find yourselves devoting your time and energies more fully to your family goals and objectives. Children have come. They clamor for special attention. Their needs must be balanced against your continuing marital priorities. Moreover, you have been advancing in your careers. You carry heightened responsibilities and have new ideas of how far you can go in the competitive world of work.

This calls for a new dimension of love and for much extra effort. Whereas two may be intimate company, even in marriage three may prove to be a crowd. It does not matter much if the third corner of the triangle is a child or a career; it can be competitive and strain the relationship.

That's when two have to work together even more fully to keep the intimacy they treasure. If their love has not matured, there will be jealousies and conflicts and the seeking of outside interests to compensate for the loss of the closeness they once so enjoyed.

There's another potential danger in this period. That is the feeling of being trapped by responsibility. Why even try to develop your creative abilities? Even if an outlet for them is recognized, there is no spare time or reserve of energy to take advantage of it.

Yet despite the extra strain—perhaps even because of it—this can be a time of great enrichment and growth. By resolutely working together to meet these new demands, you may discover new depths of love and devotion in each other that you never sensed before. Your admiration for and appreciation of your beloved grows. So does your marriage.

As children grow up, your life together takes on yet another shape. If you made the mistake of living only for your children over the past many years, this could prove quite a traumatic time. Then you well might feel an emptiness and loneliness the likes of which you never experienced before. This is commonly called the mid-life crisis.

But it does not have to be that way. Nor should it be. This is actually the time when you can recapture some of the intimate togetherness you did not have time for in recent years. You can begin to do things that you could not afford before, and you can do them at a more relaxed and enjoyable pace. In fact, your whole relationship is deeper and more relaxed. God has brought you through a lot together. You no longer have to explore and test what you can expect of each other. You know and appreciate.

Another advantage of this stage is that your increased time and somewhat diminished family demands make it possible for each of you to exercise your individuality again without threatening the other or the marriage. You can pursue long-neglected private interests and be happy with each other in the process. It's a warm and comfortable time in marriage. But it could not be if you wanted and expected your marriage to be the same as it was when you said, "We do!"

The changes thereafter are not as markedly different. Closeness becomes deeper and richer as two people become increasingly dependent on each other. Is the love and the marriage different from the exciting early years? Obviously so, but it is no less beautiful or fulfilling.

As you put the big picture together, isn't God wonderful? Can you think of any improvement on the way He made us or the way He designed marriage as a lifelong source of blessing for us? Thank Him! Praise Him! Let your whole marriage be a doxology!